Contents

MANY RED FISH
STEVE SPENCE

KFS

Newton-le-Willows

Published in the United Kingdom in 2019
by The Knives Forks And Spoons Press,
51 Pipit Avenue,
Newton-le-Willows,
Merseyside,
WA12 9RG.

ISBN 978-1-912211-23-4

Acknowledgements:

Some of these poems have appeared in the following magazines: *Stride*
(online); *Tears in the Fence*; *The Rialto*.

MANY RED FISH

An even break

Using big data to diagnose problems and predict
success is one thing. Yet there is no other path
and a key responsibility includes cooking with gas.

What's your water source? Hopefully, people will
always subvert things yet we also found that parental
consent forms were inadequately completed.

I'm not texting nobody. I can't concentrate
on the bus. There's too much noise. Just wait
'til we get to town and we'll sort it all out.

There are gasps of disappointment. He was a slow
learner but after signing his contract he spent three
months waving goodbye. Should I leave or should I stay?

When it came to materials we had some idea of what we
were after. What have they done to deserve to be famous?
Yet we prefer to identify issues and then resolve them.

There's a huge network of people with their eyes to
the ground though inevitably the brightness of a star
will gradually increase and then decrease.

"We're not looking for the bodies but for the marks
the bodies left behind," she said. Yet your overall
experience is still more than the sum of its parts.

It was a close-run thing and we remain unsure of
the implications. Peas can be frozen and will taste
delicious when defrosted. This swim is fizzing with fish.

A closed door

With her front legs resting on the surface and
her back on the reeds she waits. Like many
others we listened again to Lou Reed's music.

It's really heavy in the current. Yes, and look
at that fin. You're the one who needs to be worried.
Our only hope is to wear down our attackers.

We're lurching from deadline to deadline and
crisis to crisis. In cinema, of course, reality is fluid
yet there are some things that robots do really well.

"I'm so filled with fear and anxiety that my life
has shut down altogether." It may be something
to do with lack of oxygen. This is tougher than rehab.

Do you like jelly? When I say the entire family,
I mean everyone. How long have you been together?
Yes, he definitely sounds unstable, though.

Everyone is fearing the worst. Yet the modern city
is terrified of stasis and you're not going to notice it's
there. These are the sharks, the skates and the rays.

When exactly did humans start living together?
Now we have the 'all-clear'. Meanwhile, out back,
the opulent glass walls reflect the park.

I don't know who or where I am any more. At what
point should we get involved? You can't have Hamlet
without the prince. Why all this surveillance in the first place?

Conducting a trial

Are we looking at a good old-fashioned
moral panic here? Services will be disrupted
but surely we were always pushing the boundaries?

Even so, these assets clearly have some value.
Is she bringing out his playful side? We are
all resourceful and use what comes to hand.

What they are doing in all these places remains
something of a puzzle. "It would be even better
to see it dive under the surface," she said.

Have you always been healthy or did you make a
conscious effort to become healthy? This bleak outlook
is counter-balanced by a few encouraging developments.

I thought you liked the shadows. Of course, these
changes often appear unsettling and he plays his cards
close to his chest. "It's coming towards us," she said.

With south-west winds blowing, your attention
should be turned to the sea. Now, it seems, we
all have an assortment of colourings.

Having an architect is crucial to the success of
the project yet the story of silk isn't just about
posh scarves and stockings. It's time to go diving.

Yesterday don't matter if it's gone. Yet we rush to
judgement and are much less willing to forgive. For
now, alien oceans are a purely hypothetical concept.

A negative situation

Of course we had misgivings yet increasing
engagement is not a magic bullet. The key is
that one loop is slightly longer than the other.

Why don't fish sing? I won't go on because
you know exactly what I'm talking about and
we don't want to send out the wrong signals.

We've been watching to see how this storm
might be brewing and we need to find a smoking
gun. The clearer the sound the closer the shark.

You have no idea what she meant – no idea!
How well do you remember your early childhood?
This is an automatically generated message.

Sources close to the deal said it could be
completed within a month. "It's not often you
use a big fish to catch a small fish," he said.

These are hopeful signs and working as a team
they're almost invincible. It's possible we could
see winds in excess of eighty miles an hour.

Who told you I wanted to be a fisherman? At which
point he lowered his eyes. This is a serious storm that is
coming our way and we need people to heed our warning.

"I'm not a big fan of a mindless use of big data." Yes,
but are we talking about developing smart cities or smart
citizens? The world is heaving with tabloid appetite.

A long descent on an escalator

Why shouldn't we have pictures people want to
look at? "That's not what it said in the advertisement,"
she said. When you forage together you eat together.

It's been a haunting and eerie experience yet its exact
design is a closely guarded secret. How good of you to
come. One moment you're alive and the next you're dead.

Up to now we've been using social media to mobilise
the time-lapse teams. Everyone knows that in the long
run the house always wins. Next up – the grasshoppers.

"Despite the risk of arrest it was always worth it,"
she said. Yet they build their bodies entirely of soft
tissue. We're going to start with a quickfire round.

Were you elected or were you appointed? If we get
the timing wrong this time we'll be stranded and die.
In such a community the whole group is important.

"We have brilliant archive workers," he said. Yet living
on food from bins is better than being part of a culture
of waste. Of course, it sounds even better with these on.

"My body is out of fuel," she said. Even in retrospect, this
craving for 'something else' seems far from frivolous. Lights
twinkle in the distant hills. It looks like we're foraging again.

When gourmets gather, smart hotels are never far behind.
Each species of fish provokes a different call yet it's rare
that being ethical ever tastes quite so delicious.

At such short notice

Should we stop using the term 'wildlife conflict'?
How do you build a new city? In this situation the
views of the rank and file may have been very different.

Are our urban landscapes bland and odourless?
"I love bringing old materials back to life," she said.
Now the military are here and posing as a liberationist army.

It's there in the remorseful and self-lacerating tone yet
all of our data relies on the manufacture of reliable and
accurate instruments. Could this be an organic dysfunction?

"It might feel like a darts crowd but they're here to dance,"
she said. Are you an insider when it comes to knowing what
is cool? You never know what may happen in a duel with pistols.

Here we see an appropriation of the 'slacker' style yet
there are moments when the tide is so strong you almost
feel you are going backwards.

At night they take on a life of their own. This glow vanishes
abruptly when a planet moves behind a star. In the midst
of all this I felt the city had given up on me.

Too often the oil ends up in places that are seen as pristine
and fragile. The entire charge then drains from the cloud above.
Her painting style is fluid but her message is brutish and short.

It's not just the sea that's been eating away at the coastline.
In the midst of all this I felt the city had given up on me yet
the sea offers sensual and illicit pleasures.

In the public realm

Why do you think you've been targeted by them?
Much of his advice remains uncontroversial but
it was more of an aspiration than a deadline.

This sudden unexpected loss is devastating.
More than half the birds never make it home yet
we prize ambiguity and love to keep you guessing.

Look at that tail going in short, swift strokes. "That's
when the unsocial behaviour legislation first went through,"
she said. The leaves on the trees may act as a sail.

Regulators must also be able to control nuisance
calls yet the event was streamed live in its entirety.
"European mice have been at the biscuit in a big way."

What does it feel like at the moment? Air passengers
may face problems and we are looking at a period of
serious disruption and chaos. The incongruity is stupefying.

People are scared to speak for fear of reprisals. Yet the
process has many possible outcomes and over time, such
resistance diminishes. Explain what you mean by 'pathogen'.

There are never enough hours in a day for the 'fully-rounded'
experience yet here you have a group of patients who don't fit
this category at all. Everyone smashes a window now and again.

Not all film adaptations work and the allegations came as a
shock. Nearer-to-home his policies have not produced the
expected results. Before leaving don't forget to catch the show.

A confidential report

Suddenly, its flukes are highlighted sharply against
the sky. The next item caught him by surprise.
"This is no ordinary doll's house," she said.

Supporters of the technique were notably absent
yet the idea was to get there just as the light was
fading. "It's like a common tern with a sore throat."

What are you fiddling with at the back? As it
turned out the evidence was compelling. Could
you suggest treatment for peripheral neuropathy?

We urge all parties to accept the outcome. Is the rump
a pale straw colour and highly streaked throughout?
It was at this point that reports of abuse began to appear.

At first sight this seems an innovative idea yet few of
us have not paused to admire the beauty of a soap
bubble. Today these sounds are as readily heard in cities.

You should always aim to shoot in natural light. Yet what
was life like for those black-coated clerks? Violence is
breaking out between the newcomers and the original residents.

Here the deepest spot may well be no more than six feet deep.
We had come face to face with our dinner and we didn't like
what we saw. These paintings tend towards the huge.

Colour and shape carry the composition. "It's a damaging
narrative," she said. "When you say 'other people' what do
you mean?" We were outsiders, interlopers, if you like.

An experiment in peril

Only one question remains. Rather than being an
exclusive thing, anyone can pay to come along.
All this takes place out of sight below the ground.

Our footsteps echo on the stone. For emerging
artists this is a difficult situation yet the puffins
are easily spooked and we have to move slowly.

There are no limits to what a healthy youth can
do but where were the clocks? "There are many
ways of attaching a float to a line," she replied.

Two such errors come to light and we desperately
need some fish. "This is a place of action and of change,"
she said. These are extended periods of low activity.

Not all peaks and troughs are equal yet there are
textbooks which deal with nothing else and there really
are no limits. How does this help us understand glass?

*"Have you ever seen duelling stag beetles," she
asked. We also have a joint robotics programme.
What about the clocks? Only one question remains.*

Almost invariably it is the natural world that
comes off worse. Profitable work awaits us though
plants, of course, live on a different time-scale.

Are we going to blunder on to the edge of the precipice?
Yet the streets are deserted and deathly silent. Only one
question remains as our footsteps echo on the stone.

Rules of the game

So when do you think this rumour started?
As darkness falls the thunderstorms begin.
My hair stands on end just telling you about it.

With a huge lake to explore we motored across
to the far tree-line. A spokesman for the force
later confirmed that he said nothing of the sort.

There is no way this building will be habitable in six
weeks. Instead, he assembles fragments, broken pieces
of action, and likes to move back and forth in time.

Everything remains confidential yet dark forces
are at work. It's always worth investing in a sea
view but you should never use an open phone line.

*From the moment they laid eyes on each other, the
atmosphere crackled with sexual electricity. There's
always a little loose debris which is easy to slip on.*

Regulation has been falling behind practice in some
areas yet we have warned users against sharing their
personal details online. This is where the avenue begins.

There's an obvious question that springs to mind.
Yes but can you tell us about the electron microscope?
This way you'll have more bacon in your roll.

Smell may not be precise but it works over much
greater distances. Would you mind if we talked inside?
An average storm produces around two strikes a minute.

A bundle of something

It's good to see that somebody knows where we're
going. This is when the negotiations began to move
slowly yet sheltering under a tree may be a bad idea.

You should think about radiator positions as these
often restrict the positioning of furniture. It's a richly
harmonic and harmonious sound. Here's how it works.

Other countries have increased their jurisdiction yet
this is a voyage of discovery that everyone can make.
"Some reefs," he said, "are kinetic." This is how it works.

It's not only designers who know how to solve
problems and it's important you attend this assessment.
At this point we can leave the traffic behind.

The rhinoceros hornbill, with its huge beak, has to
be a bit of a juggler. Who are you calling functionally
illiterate? Please let us know if you enjoyed this event.

*She whispered in his ear and he led us down a spiral
staircase. How do we end up with the buildings that
surround us? Then I took a dead bird and put it on my head.*

Here's how it works. You can see it in the archaeological
record. Let's hope they don't have their claws out. Yet I
love that resin finish and the light here is very special.

Just look at how the skeleton moves. At least you're
never short of someone to blame when she's around.
Lightning may also travel down your telephone line.

Hard to navigate

Is this really a matter of equality within the law?
"It's the not-quite-knowing that keeps the spark alive,"
she said. Unlike most sand, this sand actually sings.

A port city relies on its relationships to elsewhere
yet we also found tiny particles of metal filings.
No wonder she did a runner. Shade returns to the woods.

Now the skeletal ribs rise from their watery
grave at every change in the tide. At this point,
the opportunities for misbehaving took off.

*New rules are in the offing yet there's not much we
can't deliver on our bikes. A price freeze may help. Do
we have the necessary procedures and protocols in place?*

How does this virus evolve in the human body? She
was then dragged violently across the sand and forced
into the boat. Are you voting 'yes' to independence?

Once displaced, we also enter the free market, not
as clients but as commodities. On the other hand
we rely heavily on vaccines and anti-viral drugs.

Are you an obsessive-compulsive cleaner? It's a long-
term approach but we think a more lasting one, yet the
biggest creature on the forest floor turns out to be a bird.

As it rises up into the clouds it feeds the storm yet
trees have a particular advantage when despatching
their seeds by air. Who are the men who made us thin?

Aware by now

Why is there never a big red button? It's a deep-water
fish, very much like the ling, yet we've just signed a
two-year contract and you need to step up to the podium.

Have you tried our gooseberry and green tea jam?
Our proposal turned his head though exorcism remains
their weapon of choice. Let's take another question.

When humming birds sleep, they breathe so slowly
they look as if they are dead. Is this the right room for
an argument? "It's time to start perking," he said.

What if the intelligence is less than intelligent? Here,
there are more lightning strikes than any other place on
earth. Habitat loss remains an important driver of change.

What inspired your interest in the subliminal cut? "It's
an oil-painting in 3D," she said. From each and every
angle it's a bewitching piece of mountain architecture.

History is never written by the vanquished and we've
spent too long freewheeling along this economic highway.
For ledgering or surface fishing, use a slightly shorter rod.

Is the moog back in vogue? Some people have covered their
lawn with decking and it became apparent that something was
wrong. I'm going to tell you about a dream you had last night.

Is the bill a little on the short side? Thunder rolls in the blue
distance. Is the tail 'spiky' with sharply pointed feathers?
At this point it may be time to press the button.

A cold-eyed lawyer

Travelling at near the speed of light, they hardly
interact with anything. It's an intoxicating rhythm and
suggests music. Why is there no mention of wave power?

There's no sign of the herring being pushed to the surface
yet he was a desperate man, steeling himself for the leap.
Lightning may also travel down your telephone line.

This time we may have to confront actual people instead
of looking at a sterile video game. Sometimes there
are small shoals, sometimes only individual fish.

In economic terms this is especially hazardous yet
the flow between street and fashion is constant and
goes both ways. Music pulses from a passing car.

"There are some nice red mullet around at the moment."
She spoke absently, watching him toy with the cigarette
end. As it happens we have just the assignment for you.

It sounds as though they're trying to make contact
with us again. Submerged peaks attract many species
from the open oceans yet her voice was raspy and agitated.

"I need constant stimulation," she said, "it's a bit like
being a spy." These days we have ways of speeding things
up. Immediate internment may be the least of their troubles.

An average storm produces around two strikes a minute.
Their appearance, when they emerge, gives little sense of
how complex they will become. A two-tier system is in place.

Waiting for permission

There are twists and turns and there is running through the woods yet this is a very beautiful building, a masterpiece of glass and mirrors. Sometimes all you get is the merest whiff.

When it came to shooting the sequence she was overcome with fear. I don't know what they were doing but they were making a lot of noise. Why are we throwing these fish back into the sea?

As a child he must have known these streets inside out yet many councils are now keeping files on people they think are posing a risk. Can we make an advancing army look like an empty street?

You should pay attention to these garments as you're likely to be seeing them again very shortly. If you have any medical reports you would like us to see please bring them with you.

"I'm often struck by unexpected smells which remind me of other smells," she said. There was no explosion and no fire yet dressing is splintered and sensualised, like fear and death.

This is one meeting of river and ocean where the result is anything but brackish though it's the cinema, rather than painting, which has done most to prolong the themes of the *fin de siecle*.

There was a girl on a red bicycle. Why are you looking at me so strangely? It was at this moment that the music reached its finale. Identification with her tormentor mingles excitement and fear.

"We'll fight your case on a 'no win, no fee' basis," she said. It can take a long time for a tree to die yet across the globe the degradation of the natural world continues apace.

A fork in the towpath

What if we did something to cause him to do what
he did? Inside their pods, the seeds are threatened by
dangerous enemies. Other reviewers are not so kind.

*There may be a surface level of similarity but she
couldn't possibly have known about all this stuff.
Several factors influenced his decision to stay on.*

Some people can conjure up imaginary smells and
some just can't. We urge all parties to accept the
outcome. A little stretch will facilitate easy movement.

His gesture went a long way towards exorcising
the ghosts of the past yet their basic needs go
unmet and they are trapped in their low-paid jobs.

It was later confirmed by official sources as a cloud.
On the other hand he did briefly sway in unison with
the others. Paper is secure, safe and pretty well permanent.

Sometimes democracy breaks out when you least
expect it but we continue to sip our drinks and say
nothing. The rail network is about to be shut down.

"Claims of abuse have fallen rapidly," he said. Are
there other people in the house? In return, successive
governments have imposed stringent austerity measures.

"Our industry may be very risk averse," she said. Then he
leapt from the tree, tearing his trousers in the process. Anxious
to retrieve the situation, she proceeded to shake his hand.

A spate of disasters

"You realise this is the fanciest, most carefully
assembled enigma yet put on the screen," she said.
Yet when evening falls the street collapses.

Have you any idea what these noises might be a
response to? Even when you're sleeping, the emails
keep piling up. There is no need to risk being bitten.

If the letter was a trap why go to all this trouble?
Yet there was no pause until the end of the second
act and a month's rain fell in just a few hours.

Whether brash or vulnerable, she was always arresting.
Why did you bring me here if you know who they are
already? Lightning may also travel down your phone line.

Whether this was a prediction or a command, he couldn't
tell yet the top fold, once again, forms the jaw. As a
new decade beckons they saddle up and move west.

I've never heard of a fish trying to attack someone
on land before. Less than a minute later she came out
into the corridor. A month's rain fell in just a few hours.

"Everything you say to us will be in confidence,"
he said. Yes, but do we have to hold it in a particular
way? This time we are building a new kind of monument.

"It's the wild bees, in particular, that are doing all
the work," she said. At this point there was a loud
crash in the direction of the billiard room.

Keep it coming

Do you live within sound of the sea? We couldn't get
a foothold in the game and it's really time we turned
the boat around. Five missiles appear to be in the air.

People lie down in order to rest but there are also those who
prefer to stand. Can you just talk us through what we're
looking at? It's not known how many casualties are trapped.

The air is filled with their darting shapes and high-pitched calls
yet we have allowed the disaster industries to set-up shop
inside this government. Some dangle free and keep on growing.

When the pods are fully ripe they burst and project the
seeds over a wide area. As darkness falls, the thunderstorms
begin and the engineers let their imaginations run wild.

These seeds are endowed with fleshy protrusions
yet here we are invited to see their work first hand.
Grouting turns black when colonised by fungus.

Some of these venues suit the young trees very well but
the marsh is not a place you'd want to live out of choice.
Here we have a trumpet mouthpiece connected to a bassoon.

People lie down in order to rest but there are also those who
prefer to stand. Can you just talk us through what we're
looking at? It's not known how many casualties are trapped.

There was a scuffle in the darkness around us. This shark
is a filter feeder, not an active predator like most of its
relatives. Then it was over, as abruptly as it had begun.

A word in the right ear

Look closely and the physical differences
are there. Not everyone in the audience is
happy and we are told the worst is still to come.

Now the trial has to be extended yet severe
flood warnings are in place. We all hoped that
these politics were never going to come back.

Incidents of pollution show no sign of declining
yet this larger massacre is taking place in slow-
motion. Waders will appear in numbers.

Can you please describe the lugworm? The
assessment will last for no longer than thirty
minutes and we will need access to your property.

Why are these plastic fragments not considered
hazardous? "It's probably all the fault of Frank
Zappa's *Valley Girl*," she said. We are filled with fear.

Is cancer a common cause of death in marine
animals? Now the trial may have to be extended.
"Tell me about the negative connotations," she said.

Are you braced for the storm surge? One survivor
spoke briefly to reporters. "We may need to review
our definition of clinical death," he said.

Why do you keep putting a question mark at the
end of every sentence? "He's a philatelist not a
philologist," she said. A storm is sweeping south.

A lingering message

Are we marching towards a sunlit fungal future?
Here's a tip for pole-fishing fans. For the rest of us
the drama and the violence of the sky is enough.

"Isolation breeds hostility," he said. Yet the
consciousness of rivalry was always there and
these conflicts are about different values.

Do you have any other distinguishable marks
or characteristics? Meanwhile, flights have
been disrupted and bridges closed.

Details include a light mid-grey streaking on
the chest and upper flanks yet their songs are
asymmetrical and apparently random.

"It's unethical, it's not illegal," she said. A slew of
fungal technologies is creeping out of the woodwork
while the madhouse remains firmly rooted in the past.

For too long we have looked at cities as spaces
and places yet prediction is impossible and we
need to give the mushroom an image makeover.

He rose from the table and was surprised to see
his own image in a great number of mirrors at the
same time. Ah! – we have a distinguished visitor.

Here there are ice formations that are found nowhere
else on earth yet dereliction of duty comes to mind
and new explanations of madness are being sought.

A material player

How many whale sharks are out there? By the time I
realised things were badly wrong it was too late yet
we all understand how to play with light and sunshine.

Three people have been arrested. With southwest
winds blowing your attention should be turned to the sea.
Fungal garments have even made it to the catwalk.

Was there a discussion about how the development
might go? Determined to travel light, he possessed only
a shoulder bag. Could or should things change radically?

Did you eavesdrop on my call? You may even learn how
to repair a clock. One way to do this is to create a new
genetic code but a mushroom is only the tip of an iceberg.

*By the time I realised things were badly wrong it was
too late. Yet it's worth watching just for the sultry way
her polished finger nails coax a stuck lift back into action.*

How do you go about valuing a piece of land? Alas, the
rest of the meal passed in a blur of morsels. There are some
nights when we can't even hear ourselves speak.

Even the toughest human diver can't stay down for long
but there is a serious point to this prevarication and we
spend much of our time running towards the storm-clouds.

Not many people can make a colonoscopy sound
amusing yet mutual antagonism between fungal species
has also been exploited. Are we braced for a storm surge?

'Talking of which ... ', she said

Aerodynamically, bees don't look promising. Have you
seen the man in his black hat? His vocal range is quite
extraordinary. We may soon be on course for a dream bream.

Yet every emotion has its own sound "and I'd quite like
to be the spider of leisure," he said. Another way to attack
the issue is to design more acceptable software.

Teaching your robots to chat may prove a tough challenge but
life will be easier when they can. So much depends on luck but
he's probably done a runner and you can throw away the key.

What's the purpose of this interview? Yet your blanket bench-
mark may be inappropriate and once again we're all on edge.
At least we can have a drink without having to travel.

Yes, although our European goalposts are moving and in
the end your safety may rely on whether you take a right
or left turn. Are you still confused by quantum mechanics?

"I'm speaking in astronomical terms, of course," she said.
A better analogy might be the violin, not the trumpet. When
did you last try to blend in with your surroundings?

It's an enormous privilege to be able to see a star at such
close quarters. Our reasons are likely to be complex yet
no one has noticed she can play comedy as well as tragedy.

Are we talking about runaway gravity mass here? Yet a
post-mortem examination is due to be carried out shortly.
When did you last try to blend in with your surroundings?

It's all about turning hydrogen into helium

Are we obsessed with vanity? Robbed of his ability
to create new memories, his life now exists only in
the present. Here we have the convection zone.

*What's your first memory of the house? A massive
collage of junk, it remains part art, part fire hazard.
Have you ever been plugging for bass?*

Their advance towards the capital seems to have slowed
yet the 'nuclear option' is to blow up the carcase with
dynamite. Are you thinking about the rings of Saturn?

*Here – let me hold your glasses a while. An entire ice-
sheet is on the move. "When it pulls, it will be pulling
against the rod itself," she said. Today the fish are lethargic.*

"There are spots on the sun," she said. We are being asked
to take another leap into the unknown. All the time you
were spinning me a line when I'd rather be spinning for perch.

Is this all about censoring our own history? Today the
fish are lethargic. "We're not there yet but it's within our
grasp," she said. Pull up another chair and join the party.

A giant star will mean curtains for us. You may need to
watch where other people are going yet it looks like another
locked door and they're only the tools of your trade.

"It's not in a steady state as it's clearly using up its fuel,"
she said. At this point she looked at me directly. "Yes, but
are you thinking about the rings of Saturn again," she asked.

Fencing a swordfish

Why aren't you afraid of the stranger in your house?
"I'd quite like to be a monarch butterfly," she said.
Are you still playing the air guitar after all these years?

"It's an excuse of a dorsal fin," he said. How do you
know what Jason did? We want a full public enquiry and
we want it now. Ahead of us lies three weeks in the saddle.

Statistics swirl around the room. "A colleague from work,
perhaps?" It might be a low-key end to the season but there's
a lot to be said for not knowing what you're doing.

Yes, but did you feel he was dangerously depressed? There's
plenty of scope for fun and games but we're still worried
about the wine-cooler. Do you represent a serious security risk?

It has to be a conscious decision to break free and our meeting
isn't until twelve thirty. Take a step back from the frenzy.
"Can we have both sustainability and abundance," she asked.

When it comes to time, is your brain making a fool of you?
But there's something cool about discussing a fish you caught
three decades ago and a wonderful sense of order is evident.

Which services would you like to sign up for? Yet outsider
art may be the next big craze and every piece of rubbish
deserves to be documented and archived.

As residents began to describe what had occurred, three further
explosions detonated loudly. It was a desperate semi-final, wholly
devoid of incident. When were you last in the cloak 'n' dagger?

Nearing completion

Playfully, he lunged and caught me by the shoulder.
When choosing a rose, colour should always be the first
thing on your mind. All materials should be sourced on site.

"Today I'm using a white and silver toby lure," she said.
By Thursday, rain will be pressing into eastern areas.
"You meet a lot of people in the music halls," she said.

Fishing is available on a day, week or season basis. Yes, but
what about the power of the state to investigate this data?
Could you please put your glasses on and face the audience?

Your presentation must be perfect. "Today we turn our
attention to infrastructure." At which point the pattern recurs.
"Whenever it rains this river literally turns red," she said.

Let's get back to the quiver-tipping. Yet we have dredging
and abstraction to contend with as the human brain has a facility
for off-the-wall thinking. Today we'll be fishing for barbel and chub.

Finally the rainy season arrives though it should be
pleasant enough when the sun breaks through. Was
there any sign of an intruder or a forced entry?

"One of them told me I was difficult to converse with," she
said. Suddenly, the knotweed became a national talking point
but the people who did this have no idea how to mix concrete.

"I'd rather not betray a confidence if you don't mind,"
he said. We'll be using the bow in the line as an indication.
Then the whole house of cards came tumbling down.

Statistics swirl around a room

Which of these statements do you agree with? Yet we
may be jeopardising our food security and passers-by
should be cautious. Just look at the size of its mouth.

Like the basking shark, the barrel jelly feeds on
plankton and is harmless to humans. This so-called
'dumb-walking' is a relatively new phenomenon.

When was the last radio contact? We are looking at
a large group of people who are eligible after these
changes. "This is not about sovereign debt," she said.

Without warning, the water suddenly plunges down
an open shaft. What is the Portuguese for déjà vu?
The whole process was stalked by a fear of failure.

When did you last influence the pure stream of news?
Each lake forms in a matter of days yet in the valley,
women with stove-pipe hats continue to work the fields.

These people have taken to the trees. There is a big
incentive not to kill the main attraction but your point of
view seems to have developed in an evidence-free zone.

So far there have been no fatalities. Would you like to
set up an identity parade? Which of these statements do
you agree with? Every last fish is plucked from the water.

Have you come to expose me? Modern life, it seems,
won't let us mess with time. Yet it's all about getting lost
in the music. As the net closes, the draw cord is pulled tight.

Motor cycles only

"As a rule he shoots quick and edits slow," she said. Did
you immediately recognise the significance of the shoe
box? In a rose or a sweet pea this is likely to prove a disaster.

Today we're hoping to encounter an uncontactable
tribe. It's strange how things come home to roost.
Yes, but can you remember the crime number?

Here is the oceanic white-tip. Who is on the escalator
going up and who is in the escalator coming down?
Why anyone would buy a scentless rose is a mystery.

"These sharks have an aggressive reputation," she said.
Are we seeing a return of the 'surveillance charter?'
Then he turned to the crowd and held up our documents.

Yes, but it's a slice through the city and I was only
trying to push the envelope. "You have to factor the
possibility of an attack into your daily life," she said.

It's the highly-prized feather we're after but it's really
just to get the fish rooting around. On several occasions
we fled from the tedium of the cutting room floor.

Are you alert to the signs of danger? His white trumpets are
exquisitely scented yet the surveillance laws have returned to
the headlines. One moment you're conscious – then you're not.

"Time should be banished," she said. Did you want
to spark a bigger debate? Yet you can always take off
the large claws and crack the shells to remove the meat.

The art of fishing

"I'm not going in there – I'm agoraphobic," she said.
The longer a wind blows on a wave, the larger it becomes.
"You can take the dog free of charge," she said.

Sunlight is streaming into the courtyard for the
first time in weeks. If this sounds familiar it's
because it's meant to be. Grey reef sharks gather.

*"Hello John – just a quick call. I'm on the train
to Plymouth." In time the bigger fish establish
dominance. "It's Joycean in its dimensions," she said.*

Can biological controls turn the tide in our
war on invasive plants? "It's a blow to the head,"
she said. Suddenly, suprematism is on our agenda.

Do you enjoy the immersive experience? In other
circumstances, testosterone appears to boost generosity.
Yet one such hybrid is the bohemian knotweed.

Here we have the stingray, the eagle ray and the butter-
fly ray. Suddenly the sky clouds over and the hail falls.
"We were cut off, Jodie, then we went into a tunnel."

Every ocean has its own unique wave rhythm yet if a
dragonfly lands on your shirt it may take over your life.
When it comes to sperm, it's quality, not youth that counts.

"Get this down your neck," he said. Here is what I have
in mind. It's obvious you are the aggressor in this case
yet most of the fish we catch here are red snappers.

The house that Jack built

It's hard to imagine the torture of waiting for the
wind yet the vast majority of its organism is hidden
underground. Today the fish are coming thick and fast.

What constitutes threatening behaviour? These were
angry consumers, not ideologues, but he hooked the
carp on a crab and mussel pop-up bait.

*"Wikipedia is notoriously inaccurate," he said. Yet the
shopping mall is king and this is what we call a critically
balanced bait. Loud explosions are followed by flashes of light.*

There's a particular sound to this bathroom but we also
need an acceptance that we may not have a common
history. Let's not forget the human cost of this violence.

Why does looking for something always make me
hungry? Despite its name Greenland is mainly white yet
here we see the psychological re-planning of consumption.

*"There's a fingerprint scanner which is very cool,"
he said. How long does a light bulb last? At a certain
point the markets will be saturated.*

These fishermen are well aware of the threat to
the sea birds. Is consumerism the biggest con-trick
in the book? All too often we return empty-handed.

How exactly does this hidden process happen?
These are treacherous waters but it's amazing
the size of fish you can catch in a tiny stream.

Steering clear of danger

"It was almost a nod to the punk era," she said.
In other words you are going to be on tenterhooks
with her not knowing and you just waiting to go.

We were watched very closely and very secretly
for a very long time. Where there was water before
now there is a killer whale. Nothing is attributable.

There's an incessant banging of drums. Some may linger
and some will quickly disappear. Now for the asparagus.
It may just be that we're not getting our message across.

We've got the weather, we've got the method and
now we've got the fish. What on earth is a 'holy
tortilla?' Tanks and other armed vehicles are involved.

Our new consumer paradise is due to be hit by a
hard economic fact yet another species now flirting
with a loss of mega-status is the pied-billed grebe.

Now we can put in the artichokes. There's an incessant
banging of drums. Soldiers have been challenged and
shaped by the Welsh hills. Yes, but what's our timescale?

This painting had immense shock value at the time as
it attempted to remove any trace of 'the real'. "Yet Spanish
white beans are the best in the world," she said.

*"It's not an auspicious start," she said. Is the situation
containable? Now we need to think tactics and act
strategically. "It's a secular gesture," she said.*

Anyone in the world

As the circle closes pellets of dye are dropped into
the water yet these are the high-seas and many yellow-
fin tuna are caught before they are old enough to breed.

What would sustainable living actually look like?
So far the robots get it right about two thirds of
the time yet testosterone may also influence behaviour.

Something doesn't seem right when the waves
are casting shadows. Was it a dispute with a
neighbour over a fence? It looks like a locked door.

We may have to accept that time is the ultimate
delusion. An exception might be the bluebell with
its rich, spicy smell. We have rudd and some chub.

Are you taking this investigation seriously?
Yet these debates are hardly new and a sky
burial is the ultimate homage to the mountain.

We are as exotic to him as he is to us. Does this
still mean there is power coming through? Please
don't leave before the end credits.

Like many pollinating insects, honeybees have been
in decline for years. Two hours of sampling work lie
ahead yet the more you insist the more I'll resist.

When did the seizures start? There's an incessant
banging of drums. "Music is about ears, not eyes,"
she said. It's just a story about two people in a room.

Reef madness

An average storm produces around two strikes a
minute yet I've never heard of a fish trying to attack
someone on land before. Tarantulas taste a bit like crab.

"There's a raven flying overhead – can you hear it?"
To get an idea of what to expect we have to go under-
ground yet a powerful wind can turn waves into monsters.

We'll be continuing with the joy of the guitar riff
at the weekend. Distinguishing dinner from danger
is an essential life skill in this environment.

*Have you ever been as drunk as a skunk? "It was a
textbook case of transference," he said. As night falls
we return to dry land to sleep. "It's a fly agaric," he said.*

For my next illusion I require a gold watch. These are
the hot spots where sharks converge in great numbers.
We are immediately thrust into a grand soundscape.

What brought the snakes crawling out of the jungle?
The shops are all shut and militiamen roam the streets.
Who could have inspired such an obvious character?

"I don't get chosen, I choose," she said. An hour later
he was forced to clarify our position and in haste I
dodged through a crowd of emergency workers.

Does the solar wind affect our weather? Fungi are
erupting yet sheltering under a tree may be a bad
idea. As darkness falls the thunderstorms begin.

Like no other

Do you still think she's the bees knees?
At the outset there was little to go on but
we think you've suffered a loss of memory.

"He was in the trap and screaming from the day
he took over," she said. Yes, we can make this
world sustainable but would you want to live here?

"We'll take our time and make the right decision," she said.
Yet the consensus view is that this is not a passing phase
and it looks like we're on the verge of another civil war.

Every house has its secrets but I wouldn't spend
the summer there. This time the vote is decisive
but a heat-wave is in nobody's interest.

I do feel for him, don't get me wrong, but she's
a sket. I get on with Caitlin now as it happens.
She's schizophrenic and she's going to bring you down.

Is consumer society just an old kind of slavery? At every
stage of their life fungi demonstrate how like us they are.
Yet surely it's just a natural reaction to spin the car away.

Yes, but is this a justified anxiety? "For example,
information about the smell and colour of a rose,"
she said. Salmon is the star ingredient of this dish.

It's just another feeding opportunity for him but
it's also home for a host of other life forms, as well
as being a talent we may be able to harness.

A coastal profile

Was there any actual fighting here? She's the
one who found the painting and she's the one
who's missing. When did you last play the skyline?

Obviously the ban won't apply on the boardwalk
but we think there's a real risk of an explosion.
A neglected wild pond is a wonderful resource.

*Are you going deeper into personal time? "It's all
about enhancing the resilience of our networks,"
he said, "but it sounds a bit like Eric Satie to me."*

They have taken revenge on defenceless civilians and
we are surrounded by fear. You won't find a crocodile
in your local swimming pool – maybe a frog or a newt.

Should we be planting native plant species to attract
native insects? Its melody is terrific but we'll all be
very lucky if no one is killed by the end of the day.

Here we are comparing different types of habitat
within our urban areas. It's all starting to sound a
bit Joni Mitchell now, mellow and intoxicating.

Is this the industrial sublime or an industrial blight?
Some outbreaks of rain will affect the southwest but
is this a legitimate target? We are surrounded by fear.

"We are calling for an international investigation," he said,
"and we demand they are brought to account." It may be
just a matter of singing your response to the landscape.

Making sense of toads

It's a pattern of behaviour that
happens over time but you should
always reckon with the wind-chill factor.

Is it a tablet or is it a broadsheet?
"We also need to understand the
risk of extinction," she said.

Does it feel tangibly exciting?
As night falls, the temperature
plummets. May the bottle reign supreme?

Let's just see what's happened
to your pulse. Finally, the balloon
begins to descend and our secret is out.

The night can take you anywhere yet
there's always a fog of uncertainty
and something's approaching our tent.

Was there anything you disagreed on?
Mrs Bear began to snore. Next time,
please wait until the guard opens the gate.

What is amazing is that there's very
little actual weather yet ice storms can
be lethal and this looks like a war zone.

Both sides will have expected
violations but several toads are
calling from different directions.

A splash-zone

Even shivering stops as your muscles slow
down but the man mountain is approaching the
castle. You don't want to risk going in?

Her reply is delicately worded. Yet it's all
happening everywhere at the same time
and the question has become irrelevant.

"It all blew up so quickly," he said. Many
people think there will be synchronised attacks.
What do we do when the missiles start to fall?

What difference does it make who started
the war? Yes, but how well do you walk the
tightrope? Flash floods are on the agenda again.

"Such magnificent footwork," she said. It's
not about technology, it's about music yet it
may be the age of the presenter is at an end.

Creeping complacency could be affecting
safety standards but every fisherman likes
to catch the occasional gilt-head bream.

Sunfish are amazing creatures but I'm not so sure
about these painted sculptures that are appearing
across the city. Would you like some time alone?

"All ability levels should be catered for
but this journey to the source is not to
be undertaken lightly," he said.

The island

"There's always a narrative," she said.
Deep frostbite is a one-way process and
the diary entries remain incomplete.

Our technology was useless against the
weather. "I would liken it to a Greek chorus,"
she said. Here we have the frozen forest.

This was more than the usual storm
and the blues are well and truly alive
in Ireland. The ice is extending its grip.

"What we're talking about here is words
about words," he said. Out here, blizzards
and snowstorms strike without warning.

As statistics swirled around the room,
the noise levels went up yet this may
depend on the authority of the risk function.

Is this the solar technology we've been
waiting for? What happens when wind and
cold combine? Have you seen our curly baits?

Are they talking about Robert Mitcham as
the mad preacher? We also observed that
the atmosphere was like a swirling sea.

Why don't you just tell us what you want?
We can't even find where we just came from.
Several hundred miles away a storm is brewing.

The fortress

Do either of you have the music in your head?
"It's all to do with the challenge of making a
film over a period of twelve years," she said.

If we stand by him he's a security risk. Yes,
but who's asking the others? Are you on the
other side of the argument or do you blame the city?

Yes, but if you dig deeper, there is little
real connection. "Only this morning I shouted
through an open window at a driver," she said.

Do bees prefer the inner city to the countryside?
Everyone is saying what they don't think today and
you leave us no alternative but to use other methods.

She didn't seem to have her hands on the wheel
but it's a ticking clock and we don't need any new
patients in this area. We think you're being set up.

According to the brochure she has used the
damp setting yet there must have been somebody
else and in my view it's a matter of judgement.

Let's explore the city from the viewpoint of
the wildlife that lives there. You should make it
look like a routine visit and monitor the situation.

Among the most fearsome-looking of them is
a white-throated monitor lizard from Tanzania.
Please name the group or organisation you represent.

The ship

Look at the colour of its fins. As it advances it
destroys everything in its path. We continue to exist
at the margins yet these seas are cold and storm-racked.

How do you remember that you can't remember?
Towing the carcass out to sea would be another possibility.
Why do you need to feel the blood on your body?

If you don't get a bite straight away you need to
keep feeding yet this hybrid is even more invasive
than its parents. Wind resistance has met its match.

"I've got it tattooed on my arm," he said. "Unfortunately, for
us Americans, the moral equivalence of war has turned out
to be war," he said. It's a serious storm and it's coming our way.

As you can tell, I've been obsessed with colour throughout
my life. Habitats have immune systems, just as animals do,
but wind and water are in constant contact.

What happens when the wind blows up a tempest at sea?
Much of its life is spent hidden underground yet a woodlouse
is a crustacean that has developed a terrestrial lifestyle.

Are you upsetting my operators? "It's the organised creation
of dissatisfaction," she said. Yes, but why are mushrooms
toxic? "It's an economy built on obsolescence," she said.

The hem of a sheer curtain brushes a window-sill yet it's
difficult to remember the sequence of events and you can always
drift the bait on the wind. "We exist at the margins," she said.

Lightning Source UK Ltd.
Milton Keynes UK
UKHW040618291019
352508UK00001B/63/P